Sandy's Legacy
Bobwhite Quail in Art and Tale

By
Kent S McManigal

Dedicated to the memory of my pet quail, Sandy
1977-1983

Photo of Sandy, in my hand.
Photographed by my grandfather, Charlie G. Hromas

Foreword

I had wanted a pet quail since the time my parents read me
That Quail, Robert by Margaret A. Stanger.

My first attempt, trying to hatch bobwhite quail eggs in a
tiny plastic bubble of an incubator, failed. I ended up
eventually hatching a chicken egg and detoured into
having a wonderful pet chicken, Eggy, for a few years.
She died too soon during the months I was incapacitated
due to a very bad bicycle accident. My desire for a pet
quail never went away.

I kept a pair of quail in a pen in the backyard, but they
were not tame and only tolerated me suspiciously. They
did however provide me with fertile quail eggs.

Finally, in the spring of 1977, when I was 13 years old, I
managed to hatch a quail egg. I named the chick "Sandy"
for the sandy-brown color of some of its down, and
because that was a very "unisex" name.

Unfortunately, *this* Sandy was to meet with tragedy only a
couple of weeks into life. My pet chipmunks escaped and
killed the chick. I was crushed.

However, my penned quail kept laying eggs and I gave it
another try almost immediately.

On my 14th birthday, June 18th, 1977 my second quail egg
hatched and "Sandy 2" came into the world. Being ever
the young scientist and artist, I documented her growth
(although I didn't yet know Sandy was a "her").

For the next 6 years, Sandy went with me almost everywhere. She was taken to school, to the barber shop (the *what*?), on vacation, and camping. She traveled from Arkansas to New Mexico, and many places in between. She put up with, and occasionally made friends with, countless other animals that I raised.

She even got "broody" a couple of times, and once I let her set on an egg which came from her parents. She hatched out her own brother, who worshiped her as "Mom" while she tried her best to ignore him. He eventually grew up and left to live the life of a wild quail.

Sandy died in my hands just weeks short of our birthday; her 6th and my 20th. Her last few weeks had shown a mental deterioration. I suppose it was to be expected since bobwhites normally live only a year and a half in the wild.

This collection of sketches, drawings, and "field notes", all of which date from that time, is what resulted from observing Sandy's life and behavior, as well as a general obsession with the bobwhite quail that followed me for many years.

I have also included a few actual photographs of Sandy to show her personality.

I hope you get to know the Sandy I loved from this collection.

This is the original cover I have had on this collection of drawings for many years. Do you think "white-out enhancements" will ever catch on?

By :
Kent
Mc Manigal

August - September
1977

This is the original "publication date", along with my "signature".

Life Stages and growth of the Bobwhite Quail (Colinus virginianus)

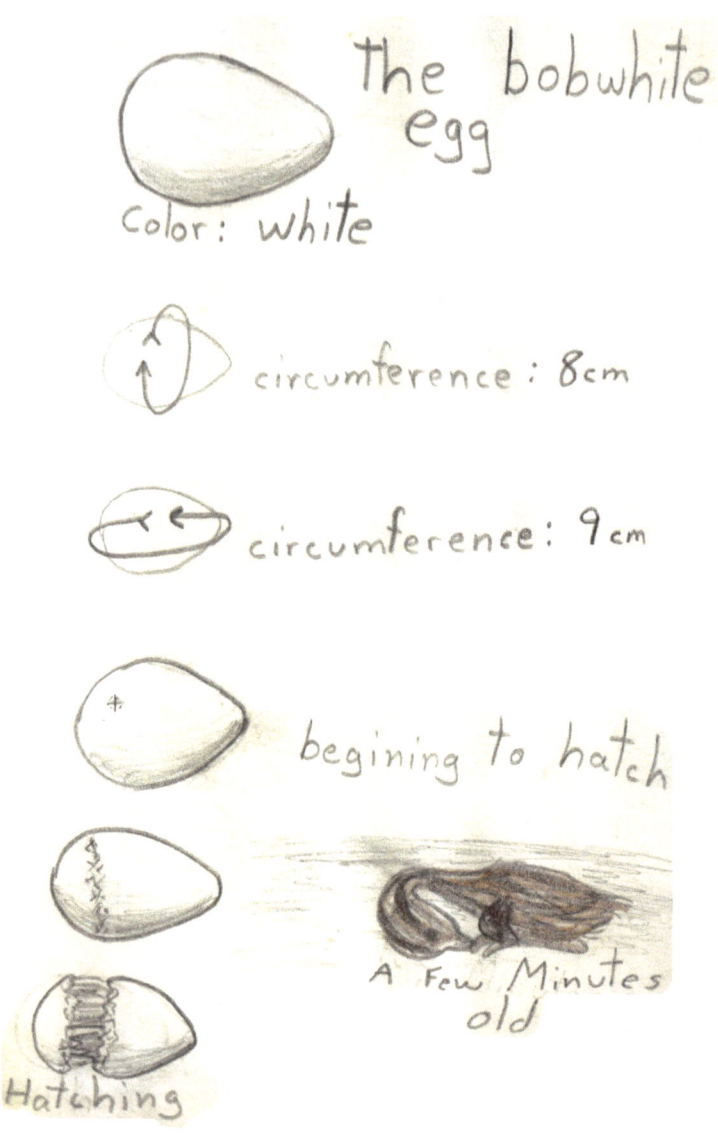

the bobwhite egg

Color: white

circumference: 8cm

circumference: 9 cm

begining to hatch

A Few Minutes old

Hatching

Yes, I misspelled "beginning". This is the "unspellchecked" truth.

Eggs, Incubation, and Hatching

Incubating eggs give off a distinctive odor. It isn't unpleasant, but touches me emotionally in the same way the smell of a baby does. Then, when it begins to hatch, the smell of the egg changes.

About the only good thing about the plastic bubble incubator was the view it permitted of the hatching egg. All children should get to experience that sight at least once.

The struggle to hatch is one of those things that makes you hold your breath. It is a life-and-death struggle, and the chicks that survive are exhausted when they finally kick out of the shell. Amazingly, most of them *do* make it out.

Sandy didn't actually hatch in the plastic incubator with the good view, but in my next-door neighbor's nicer metal incubator. It had better temperature control and was more reliable. But this also meant I didn't get to watch Sandy hatch as I had watched other birds.

These drawings were composites of the many different hatchings I watched.

The Chick

Once the chick recovers from the work of hatching, and begins to fluff up, there are few animals more adorable.

A quail chick is about the size of a "superball", but fuzzy. When they run across the floor, on legs too small to see in action, the chick looks like a ball of fluff rolling around.

Almost immediately, the chick begins to change. Daily you can see the difference as it gets stronger, more confident, and within days the pin feathers begin to pierce the baby-down.

At this size, I let Sandy hop into my mouth a couple of times. Strange, I know. I suppose she liked the dark warmth. I feared that she would choose that moment to leave a dropping.

She was without fear around me. Once, as I held her, she walked off my hand and landed in a glass of water I had been drinking from. I quickly scooped her out, dried her off, and she was just fine. It gave *me* a scare, though.

I subjected Sandy to the indignities of being measured.
Not an easy task. Probably, if I'd had access to a scale that
weighed in milligrams, she would have been weighed as
well. It was my idea of scientific documentation.

I also turned the living room into an unofficial bobwhite
museum for a few months at one point. Probably the
least-visited museum to ever exist. I think *one* of my
friends actually "toured" it once.

1 Week-old
Bobwhite
Quail

6 cm tall

At this age, the chick has already lost the "ball of fluff" look to a close observer. Pin feathers are peeking through the down on the wings and tail. They look like dark gray plastic sticks with a tiny puff of down on the tip. This "stick" cracks open eventually and a feather, which was developing inside, almost blooms as it takes shape.

Sandy was very attached to me. If I was out of her sight she would start calling with the distinctive cry of a lost chick. The call consists of rather loud chirps that rise in pitch, much like a question. It is the chick's way of saying "*Mommy! Where did you go?*"

She followed me all around the house and all over the yard. She also blended in to our carpet and the leaf litter and it took a lot of attentiveness and concentration to avoid stepping on her.

Every little speck had to be investigated and pecked at, just in case it might be food. She ate many things that were only marginally "edible". Even a chick has the instinct to eat bits of rock and gravel in order to help digest its food. She was eating commercial chick starter mostly, but was trying out anything that looked interesting, too.

By the time the chick is two weeks old, the wing feathers really have begun to look like short feathers. Little hopping attempts at flight start to occur. Stretching, fluttering exercises where the chick flaps her wings and stands on tip-toes become more frequent.

Pin feathers are starting to show up in other body areas, too.

In her first two weeks Sandy had almost doubled in size, and her personality was developing.

2 Week-old
Bobwhite
Quail

8 cm tall

3 week-old Bobwhite
Quail

10 cm tall

Now, at three weeks old, the chick has little feathers on the crop area. The crop is a sack at the base of the bird's neck that holds food after being swallowed, but before it goes into the stomach.

Why did I always draw the chick facing the same direction? I still have trouble breaking the mold once I have drawn something facing one direction or the other.

At four weeks, the chick has lost the "chick look" and looks more quail-like. From this point on is the "scruffy adolescent" stage.

I don't seem to have taken many pictures of Sandy during this time.

4 week - old
Bobwhite
Quail

11cm tall

5 Week-old
Bobwhite
Quail
12 cm tall

The feathers of the quail's crest are very expressive. They are almost like a person's eyebrows and show surprise or interest. If the crest rises, you know something has caught her attention. Then, if the thing turns out to be scary, the crest quickly flattens and the quail will dart for cover.

The "darting for cover" instinct, which is really more like scooting or shuffling for cover, was amusing when Sandy would be riding in the car. She preferred to ride either on the dash or sitting on the back of the front seat. Anytime we drove under a bridge or even past a tall object, her "*It's a HAWK!*" reflex would make her scoot sideways in a flash. Of course, there was nothing for her to scoot under, but it seemed to satisfy her.

If she became too upset she would leave a black, tarry dropping that smelled terrible. Being trapped in the car with that smell was rather unpleasant. It was also very hard to clean off the carpet at home. Her normal droppings were much less smelly and were easy to pick up. Yes, I spent much of my time cleaning quail droppings off the floor at home. Sandy was worth it. My parents didn't really want the house to turn into a chicken coop, so I did my best to keep her messes picked up.

Each week, as the quail grows, you think "*now this looks like a 'real quail'*", only to realize later how much more growth and development were remaining at that point.

As Sandy grew, I began to feel better about letting her have her "dirt time" in the back yard out of my sight.

Once, while camping, Sandy was roaming around as we broke camp (if that's what you call it when you roll down your pop-up trailer).

Unfortunately, just about the time we were ready to leave, it started to rain. Sandy didn't like getting wet so she took shelter under a bush. I needed to find her so we could leave, but she didn't answer my calls.

I'm sure the campground residents wondered about the odd family all wandering around their campsite whistling and looking under bushes.

Sandy finally appeared, unconcerned as ever. And a lot drier than the rest of us.

6 Week-Old
Bobwhite
Quail
13 cm tall

7 Week-Old
Bobwhite
Quail
14 cm tall

Sandy's home was a 10 gallon aquarium with a screen top. She slept in there at night, and was put in it anytime I had to leave her. She did not sleep well if there was the slightest hint of light at night, so I learned to do without a nightlight.

If she was in her house and wanted out, she would peck at the glass until I took the lid off, then she would hop to the rim, look at the floor, and carefully hop down.

Then would come the hopping, jumping, and flapping. This was how she stretched after being cooped up. She would flap and hop in crazy circles around the room for a few moments, then she would usually come over to me for a visit.

I normally left the lid off her house while she was out. When she got hungry or thirsty, she would hop back in for a snack. Sometimes she would even take a short nap while there. She preferred the area beside the sliding glass door for her naps, though. She liked the view, and she loved the warm sunshine.

If Sandy wanted to go outside she would pace against the glass door, pecking at it until someone opened it for her. Then, like a cat, she would step halfway out and pause. She'd crane her neck to look around and see what was out there. Then, when she was ready, she'd step out onto the porch and begin her outdoor routine, which never varied unless she was interrupted.

Many times she would be outside alone for several hours. If she got ready to come back in before someone (me) went out and whistled for her, she would come back to the sliding door and peck at the glass until someone heard her and opened the door again.

We should *all* have such a life.

2 Month-Old Bobwhite
Quail
14 cm tall

10 Week-old Bobwhite
Quail
16 cm tall

When people met Sandy, the most common question was *"How do you keep her from running away?"*

I didn't. Sandy could have left at any time. She stayed only because she chose to stay. People didn't understand how relaxed she was and how content. Few dogs or cats are any more a part of the family than was Sandy.

A wildlife photographer once came to our house and followed Sandy around the yard and through the woods taking photographs of her. He said he enjoyed the opportunity to get to take pictures of a quail that was completely relaxed and unconcerned about his presence. She acted completely naturally, because it wasn't an *act*. She was just herself doing what she always did.

I still have a couple of wildlife magazines with pictures of Sandy in them. Fame didn't go to her head, perhaps because she was happily anonymous.

A couple of times people would ask to hold her, and then they'd grip her like they thought she would try to escape. And then, of course, she *would* try to get out of their grip. She lost a few feathers in an incident like this once. After that I was much more cautious about who got to hold her, and everyone got a more thorough lesson first.

When Sandy was still growing, I hoped it would turn out that Sandy was a male.

The male bobwhite has beautiful patterns of crisp white and black on his head. His beak is a much prettier color than that of the female, too. And of course, only the male makes the distinctive "ah bob-WHITE!" call.

However, I don't remember even the slightest disappointment when Sandy was old enough that it was obvious she was female.

Adult Bobwhite
Quail
18 cm tall

(Male)
(Female has tan
color on head
Instead of
white.)

It is apparent to me that I copied this from somewhere. It isn't a drawing of Sandy, since this quail is male. And, it isn't quite my normal "style", either.

Life of a Bobwhite

1 day
4.5 cm

1 week
6cm

2 weeks
8 cm

3 weeks
10 cm

4 weeks
11 cm

This page, and the next two pages, show my attempt to "do it *again*" after I had already drawn the pictures of the quail growth stages that appear on the previous pages. For this attempt I also put multiple images on each page.

I'm not sure they are much better, but they are a little different. I include these for comparison.

32

Life of a Bobwhite (continued)

5 weeks
12 cm

6 weeks
13 cm

7 Weeks
14 cm

2 Months
15 cm

10 weeks
16 cm

34

These are all actions you will see many times a day if you spend time around quail, or in some cases, chickens.

Here is Sandy in 1978 with her chick, Bobby, behind her. The yard was her domain.

In this picture you can see why, if you didn't know where to look, and if she was being quiet and still, you would have a very hard time seeing her among the natural ground cover.

Many times I walked right past her without seeing her until she either moved or called out to me with her soft, contented "cluck".

Sandy taught me to speak fluent bobwhite. I can still call quail right to me using the calls she taught me. There were several times I sat very still and called a quail to within a few feet before it got suspicious and slipped away.

To this day, if I hear the soft sounds of a quail in the field, I know exactly what mood it is in and often what it is doing by the sounds it is making.

I'm not sure if Sandy *enjoyed* going camping; to her it may have all been the same old thing.

This was the "box" that we *all* stayed in when we went.

This box with a window was *Sandy's* travel home. In it, she went to school with me on several occasions, as well as many other places.

Here she is on a camping trip, enjoying the sunshine.

The time we took her and Nibby the baby cottontail rabbit camping was fun. Other campers had never seen a quail and a cottontail hanging around camp and so happy to be with people.

Sandy felt right at home wandering around the house. She acted like a queen. You can almost see her attitude here.

Sandy, in her prime. April 26, 1979 This is how I will
always remember her looking.

When Sandy would be out in the backyard, which was really just the edge of the woods, and she got lonely, she would start giving the call that a bobwhite makes when it has lost its covey. This is a very loud, piercing call.

Wild quail from the woods would answer her. Since I answered her in the same way, she would keep calling and the wild bobwhite would seek her out. Usually it was a male rather than the female portrayed here.

The hopeful quail would approach Sandy and she would ignore him until he got too persistent. Then she would peck him and chase him off, sometimes flying behind him until he was far into the woods.

Then, when she felt he had gotten the point and wouldn't follow her again, she would land and take her sweet time strolling and browsing her way back home. This could take a couple of hours.

If I needed her home more quickly, I would whistle the "lost quail call" and she would come flying through the air to land near my feet within a few seconds.

For fun, we would race. If we were out in the woods or at the back of the property together, and I suddenly started running as hard as I could toward the house, she would wait until I had a big head-start, and then would leap into the air and fly right past me. She would be waiting on the back step when I got there. She *never* lost.

When my penned quail got more numerous I got to see them sleeping in "covey formation". This is how the wild bobwhites I would find in the woods and fields would be resting. In this position they can explode into flight if they get disturbed without running into one another. This explosion of quail can nearly cause heart attacks in hikers, too.

Back when I only had a pair of bobwhites, I would often see the pair sleeping this way. When Sandy was raising the chick, and it got much closer to her size, they would sometimes sleep like this.

In fact, Nibby the baby cottontail used to nap beside Sandy in this way. She tolerated it, but looked uncomfortable. The rabbit looked very content.

Here are Sandy and Nibby the rabbit, back when Nibby
was *very* small.

Sandy is apparently napping, but Nibby is awake.

Most chicken-like birds, including quail, love to dirt bathe. This involves scratching a spot in the dirt until it becomes dusty, then fluffing the dust through her feathers to absorb oils and knock out dandruff and old feathers.

When Sandy stepped out the back door, she would head fairly straight, with only minor detours for pecking at interesting food possibilities, to her favorite dirt bathing spot at the base of a big pine tree, just about 20 feet from the door. The dirt bath normally took 15 minutes or so. Then she would stand up, shake all the dust out of her feathers, and be ready to find things to nibble on.

She also dirt bathed in plantless flower pots on occasion. I once tried keeping a box of good dirt for winter, or rainy weather, use, but my sister's cat decided it was a spare litter box. I didn't discover this until too late. Sandy smelled pretty bad for a few days after *that* bath.

Here is another, more "artistic" version of a dirt-bathing bobwhite.

This is the stage of the bath where the quail rolls onto his side and slowly pushes the dirt aside with the lower leg, relishing every moment. No human in a hot tub ever looked more content.

Female and eggs

This is another picture I suspect I copied from somewhere.
It does give a good idea of what a mother bobwhite looks
like with her chicks nestled in her feathers.

Sandy looked much more annoyed when she was raising
her one and only chick. I loved her, but she was *not* the
best mother.

I am positive I *had* to have copied this picture from something I was looking at. It is much too good for my work.

I did copy well, though, didn't I?

Now, this is more like *my* normal style. Notice the
agitation depicted by the raised crest. And the ruffled
feather on the neck. The more I look at this quail, the
more it reminds me of a phoenix.

Here is my illustration of a bobwhite preening. This usually came soon after the dirt bath, and several other times a day as well.

If I held Sandy, she would feel the need to preen afterward to get her feathers back in place. With her beak, she would squeeze the oil gland on her back, near her tail, to collect oil that she would then spread over her feathers. I suppose it kept them water-resistant although *I* couldn't tell.

Many times you could find where she had been sitting to preen, because of the tiny feathers she would shed, and by all the feather dandruff. New feathers are encased in a sheath, and during preening the sheaths are picked off the maturing feathers. This looks like bad dandruff and could make quite a little mess at times.

Fortunately she only grew a lot of new feathers every six months, during her moult. During this time she would have a porcupine-like appearance due to all the pin feathers sticking through her other feathers. Especially on her head where the other feathers were small and short.

Sunning

This is another "spa activity" that Sandy enjoyed. Indoors she would find a sunbeam and lie on the floor soaking it in, like a cat. Outdoors she would do this on a cool, but sunny, day when she had finished her explorations. I really think she preferred to do this inside, on the carpet. She might have been a little bit spoiled.

The quail's wing, with its gray flight feathers, always made me think of a solar panel as she spread it over her legs and lay on her side. I have to admit, it looked like it felt very good.

Have you ever seen a quail in a more noble and
intimidating pose? Me neither.

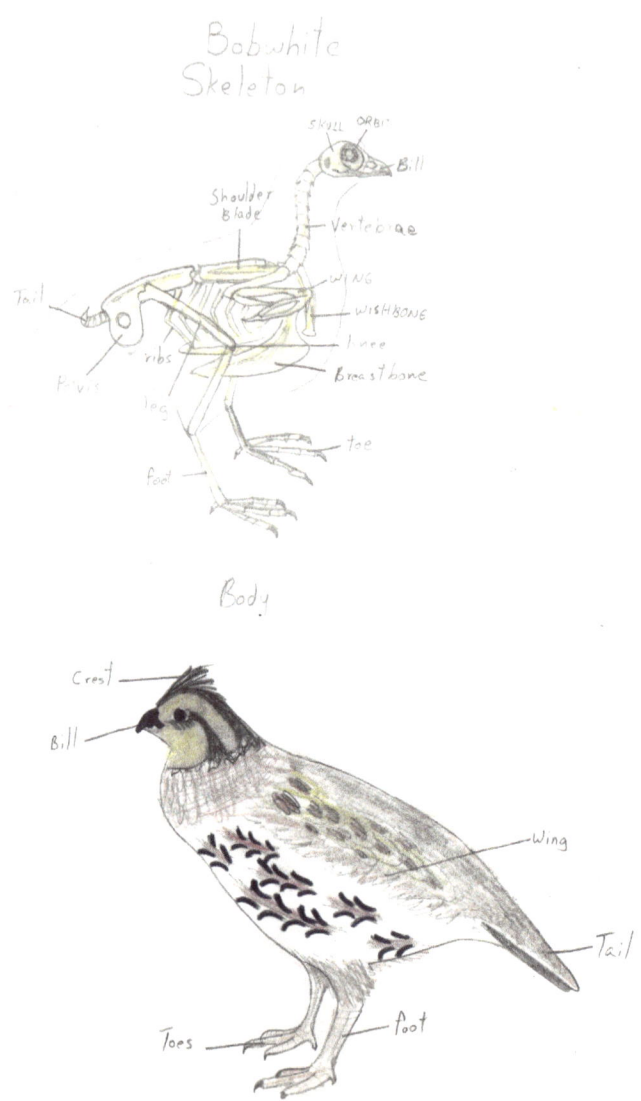

Bobwhite Skeleton

SKULL ORBIT

Bill

Shoulder Blade

Vertebrae

Tail

WING

WISHBONE

knee

ribs

Breastbone

Pelvis

leg

toe

foot

Body

Crest

Bill

Wing

Tail

Toes

foot

Yes, I *did* actually have a bobwhite skeleton for a while that I assembled myself. I wouldn't count on scientific accuracy here, especially where the number of ribs or vertebrae are concerned.

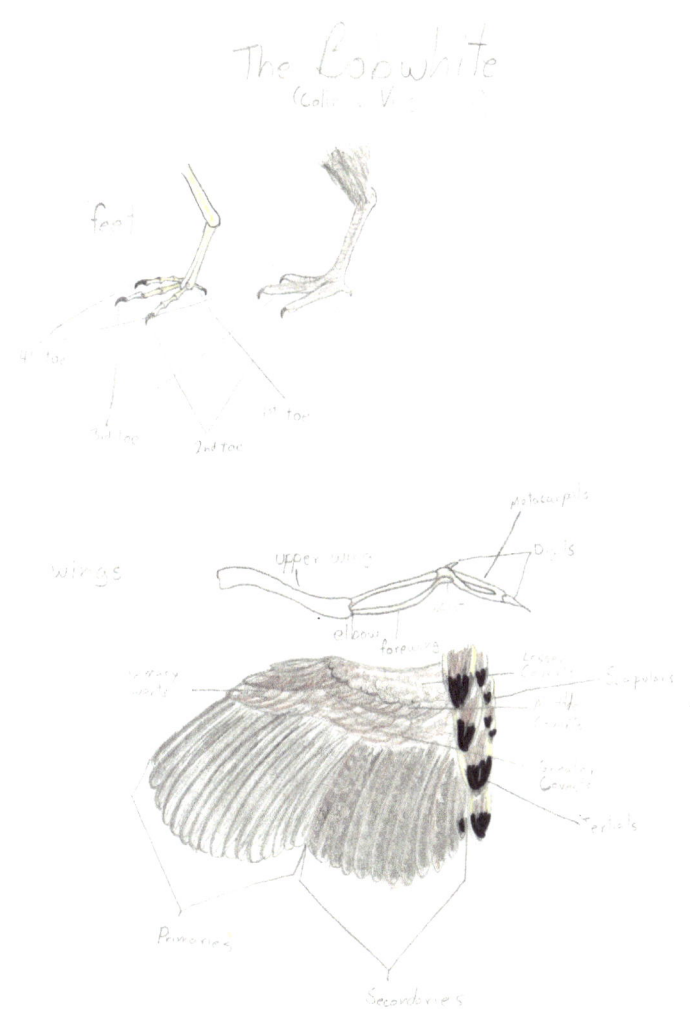

The Bobwhite
(Colinus V...)

feet

4th toe

3rd toe

2nd toe

1st toe

wings

metacarpus

Digits

upper wing

elbow

forearm

primary coverts

Scapulars

Greater Coverts

Lesser Coverts

Tertials

Primaries

Secondaries

I suppose I wanted to know bobwhites inside and out. I
tend to try to get to the bottom of anything I become
interested in, and only give other things a cursory glance.
Maybe it is because I understand life isn't long enough to
know everything about everything and we all must choose
those things that are most important to us.

This is Sandy fluffing her feathers back into place after being handled. This is also what she did after a dirt bath to shake out all the dust and debris.

Quabbit

A "quabbit"? This one is just for fun. I often like to imagine what a combination of different animals might look like. I suspect I drew this while raising Nibby, the cottontail that followed Sandy everywhere she went for several weeks.

I hope you enjoyed this journey down memory lane with me. I know *I* enjoyed it. I also hope you learned something along the way.

I had always wanted to do something with the quail drawings I had made back during Sandy's lifetime, and I also wanted to memorialize Sandy in some way.

This book let me do both. Thank you!

Also by Kent S McManigal

Indy-Pindy The Liberty Mouse
An introduction to liberty, responsibility, and independence for young readers.

Kent's Liberty Primer
A handbook for understanding Liberty and rights, and why they matter.

Contact me at: dullhawk@hotmail.com

As long as I am alive, online, and email formats don't *change*, I will keep this email address.

www.ingramcontent.com/pod-product-compliance
Lightning Source LLC
Chambersburg PA
CBHW040324010626
45792CB00024B/2117